D1061073

45 Year Memorial Photo Album

ARROW
ROLLOUT

October 4, 1957

Arrow Rollout

45 Year Memorial Photo Album

Canadian Cataloging in Publication Data

ISBN 1-55056-902-3

Main entry under title:

Arrow Rollout
45 Year Memorial Photo Album
Includes index.
ISBN 1-55056-902-3
1. Arrow...Aviation
2. Rebuilding...History, Canada
3. Photo Collection
1.†Avro Arrow (Turbojet fighter plane)--Pictorial works.
I.†Title.
TL685.3.Z879 2002 623.7'464 C2002-905233-5

First Printing, October 2002

Design by Peter Zuuring & Jozef VanVeenen
Typesetting and Layout by Jozef VanVeenen
Cover Design - Jozef VanVeenen
Photo Editing/Retouching - Jozef VanVeenen
Editing - Essence Communications

Printed and Bound in Canada by Friesens

Contact Us

62 North Street,
Kingston, Ontario K7K 1J8
Phone/Fax: (613) 531-4156
Direct E-mail: arrowz@attcanada.ca
Web E-mail: director@arrow-alliance.com
Website: arrow-alliance.com

The Arrow Alliance and its subsidiaries / affiliates are official licencees of the Canada Aviation Museum in Ottawa. Furthermore the Alliance has permission from Magellan Aerospace Ltd., Malton, for the use of the Avro Aircraft and Orenda Engines logos as well as permission without recourse to use of the photos presented. Even though ownership of the Hawker Siddeley photo negative collection was transferred to the National Aviation Museum in Ottawa, in the early nineteen nineties, any residual copyrights that Magellan Aerospace may have acquired through their acquisition of Orenda Engines Ltd. have been kindly waived and confirmed by our photo reproduction agreement with the Canada Aviation Museum of Ottawa.

Summer 2002

The Story of the Photos

NATIONAL AVIATION MUSEUM
OTTAWA

RECEIPT: The object(s) below has (have) been received by the National Aviation Museum

From: Hawker Siddeley Canada
3160 Derry Road East
Mississauga, Ontario
L4T 1A9

For the purpose of: LOAN [ ] DONATION [X] PURCHASE [ ]
TAX RECEIPT [X] EVALUATION [ ]
EXHIBIT/ARTICLE(S) [ ]

Conditions of Agreement (if evaluation state period and responsibility for return)
Permanent Ownership By National Aviation Museum

Received by: Date:

Item(s)	Remark(s)
14,000 approx Negatives 600 approx Prints (Nobel) 19 Films	Make VHS Copy + Return to John Armstrong

I accept these conditions.
This 23 day of April 1992.
1-416-673-4041

Please accept this form in lieu of an invoice.
Date: 23 Apr 92
Object(s) returned to owner.
Date:

The actual delivery/acceptance document that proves Hawker Siddeley Canada Ltd. transferred ownership of the 14,000+ historical photo collection to the National Aviation Museum, in the early nineties, for a tax receipt and safe keeping.

Early in 2002 I found out that the Canada Aviation Museum in Ottawa had acquired more than 14,000 photo negatives from Hawker Siddeley Canada Ltd. in the early 1990s. These recorded many aspects of the former A.V.Roe Canada Ltd umbrella organization that included Avro Aircraft Ltd. and Orenda Engines Ltd. They are stored in many small boxes and drawers in several places around the museum.

Some sorting of these negatives had been done by volunteers soon after their acquisition but only in a global way. I became a registered volunteer and got the task of continuing this process. Was I in for a surprise! Day after Day I stared, like a radiologist, at the lightbox - passing my loop over the 4 X 5 inch negative with obvious delight, sometimes boredom and yes, 'Eureka!' at times.

After several months I isolated approximately 3,000 negatives that applied directly to the Avro Arrow and Orenda Iroquois developments. Further sorting into Avro and Orenda, then into development, manufacturing, operating, ceremonial/events, people, and then further subsets of these, led to being able to pick about 360 really superb photos. These photos relate to important events that tie into a 45 year memorial possibility. They are the Arrow's rollout, the Arrow's first flight and the Iroquois' rollout...yes there was an Iroquois rollout celebration albeit with less fanfare than the Arrow. Many of these were new to me and a delight to behold.

BGM imaging in Ottawa is the designated photo processing house for the museum. After some time/price negotiations with BGM's vice-president Rip Jones, the negatives were supplied in three batches. Paul Latreille , their experienced darkroom man, was assigned to the job. Both BGM and Paul are to be commended for the effort they put into this project. One never knows the quality of the positive that comes from an old negative. Many times several exposures were made in order to balance grey scales and saturations of black and white so that later computer scanning would have the best possible result. Furthermore, the work was completed in record time.

The quality of BGM's work coupled with the photo retouching skills of Joe Van Veenen, our Graphic Designer, gives you these wonderful snapshots of an unforgettable period in our aviation history.

Peter Zuuring,
Kingston, ON, Fall 2002

FORM 587 A Nº 74891

NEGATIVE IDENTIFICATION

DESCRIPTION: Do Not Print
As per RCAF

ORIGINATED BY:
TAKEN BY: DOCKET No:
DATE: DOCKET DATE:

It is curious that some photo negatives included the comment, " Do not print, as per the RCAF." What was special about their content that would necessitate that comment?

A. V. Roe Canada is firmly entrenched at Malton as the new Avro Aircraft Limited subsidiary sign "AVRO" is mounted on the main administration building central tower. The top floor was the company's boardroom.

Introduction

It is with great pleasure that I present this Limited Edition 45 Year Memorial Photo Album of the Arrow's Rollout for your viewing pleasure.

I have been digging out the Arrow story for five years. Along the way I have found amazing things and met many fantastic Canadians some of whom had the honour and thrill of working at Avro or Orenda directly during those heady days in Malton. Finding the photos that you are about to peruse has been particularly delightful. Lou Wise and his Avro photo crew did such superb work that their efforts look as fresh today as they did then.

Serendipity got the Arrow Scrapbook on its way when I met Jan Zurakowski by accident during my first closed door visit to, the then, National Aviation Museum. Similarly, key documentation from Avro's official Arrow Rollout Ceremony came my way through an old Lorne Park High School classmate of my older brother. One night I got a call from a Michael Jenkyns asking me if I was that Peter Zuuring that attended Lorne Park High School in the late fifties and early sixties. I said "Yes, I was." Then he told me who he was and further related that his father, Stan Jenkyns, was head of Avro security during the Arrow period and that he had stuff in his basement. Would I come over and have a look? You bet I did! The Rollout VIP folder, speeches, and brochures came straight from this source. How lucky we are to have them to round out our visual journey. Likewise the Globe & Mail and Toronto Star cutouts, that put the event in perspective, were supplied by the Jenkyns' family. Thank you!

The captions for the photos are made out to the best of my ability Sometimes limited sources of information make identifying people, places, processes and/or parts difficult. If you, the reader, have information relating to these photos and the Rollout event that correct or compliment our effort please contact us at the Arrow Alliance.

For interest I have included the security badges that belonged to Stan Jenkyns. Note how he had the only badge in the plant that indicated the cleared employee's name but was also authorized by the same person... Mr. Stan Jenkyns.

Jim Floyd proudly displays the McCurdy Trophy, the annual Canadian Aeronautical Institute award of merit for outstanding achievement in the field of aviation. It's 1958 — it's for his work on the Arrow.

James C. Floyd,

Winner of Canada's top aviation award, The McCurdy Trophy, sponsored by the Canadian Aeronautical Institute.

Jim Floyd is a quiet unassuming gentleman whose demeanor hides the tremendous contributions he has made to the world of supersonic flight. Building a career that spans decades included significant time at Avro Aircraft Ltd., first as Chief Engineer and later as Vice-President of Engineering.

During his early tenure at Avro's Malton plant Jim designed and built the famous Jetliner, Canada's first regional commercial jet. Next on Jim's list of achievements shows that he worked through and shepherded many of the CF-100 fixes, some say thousands of engineering changes, that finally made the Clunk the success that it became. Close to 700 jet fighters, through five versions, were produced.

When it came time for the RCAF to choose a successor to the CF-100, Jim played a significant part in converting those agreed to new tough specifications into a buildable, modern, supersonic jet interceptor/fighter. In record time wind tunnel models confirmed the shape that we have come to love as the Arrow. Jim Chamberlain's aerodynamic expertise and magic created a shape that slipped through the air. When the MKI flew some four years later, it nearly reached its design speed limit with the lower powered Pratt & Whitney J-75. We can only imagine what might have been with the Orenda Engines Iroquois.

The format of this Rollout Memorial Photo Album follows Avro's publication format on the subject. You will see rare photos of the wooden mockup interior as the metal mockup takes shape, arrow component sections are constructed and assembled to form the completed aircraft and finally you are there. It's October 4, 1957.

The Arrow rolls out today. Follow the entire sequence of events from step by step photos to copies of Fred Smye's, Hugh Campbell's and George Pearkes' speeches while the assembled thousands stand by.

Jim Floyd was there...what memories remain.

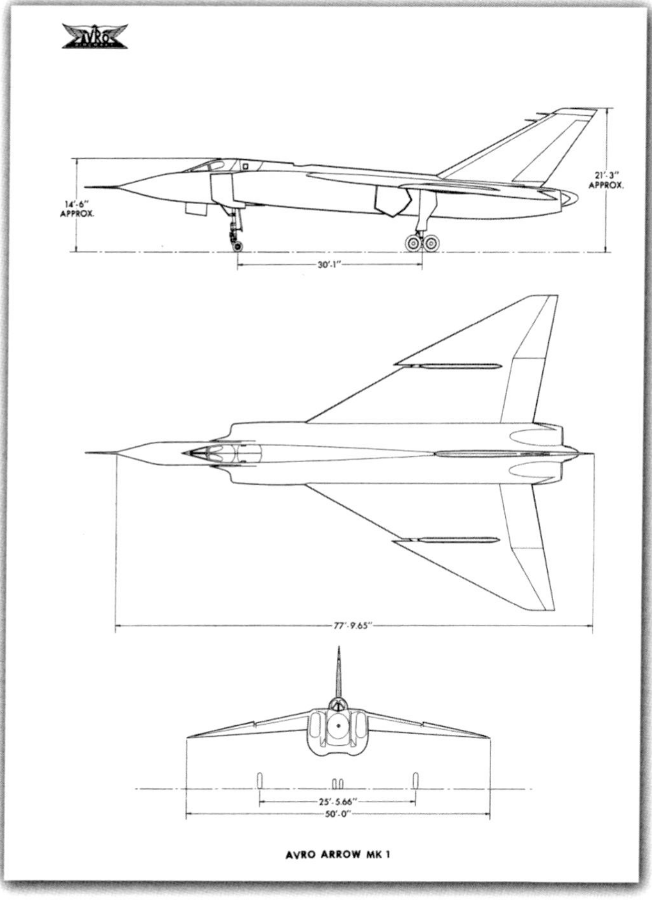

The wooden mock-up in the experimental building, D-1, is being transformed from the MKI to the MKII version. The Iroquois engine mock-up is clearly visible at point of entry near the exhaust nacelles.

The mock-up had only one wing which was supported by wires from the ceiling. Large scale Engineering Conferences were held for each of the MKI and II versions. The RCAF had ample time to explore, comment, and suggest as the design evolved.

An oblique view of the pilot position. The long pipe in the bottom left of the photo is the ejection seat explosive driving mechanism.

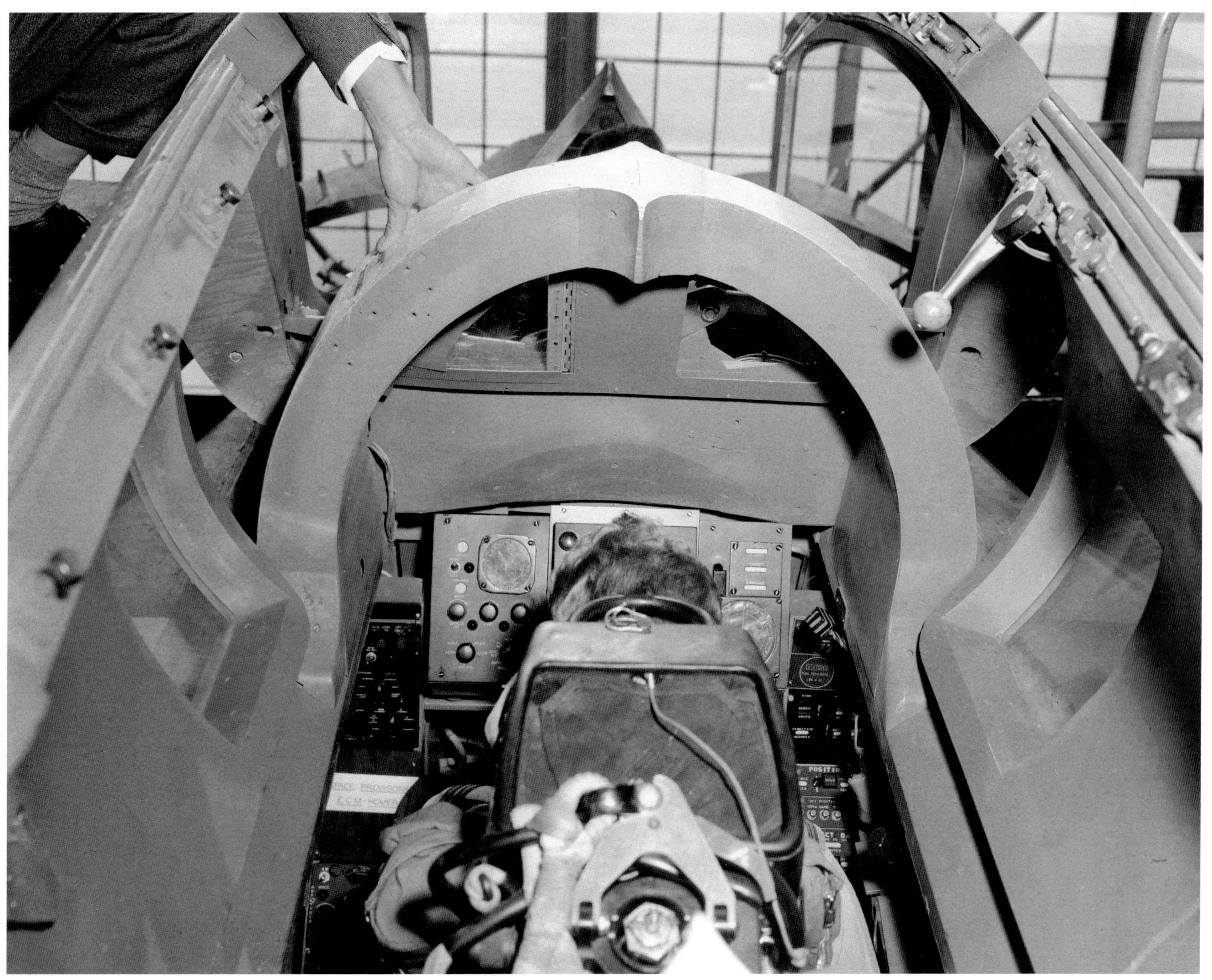

Looking forward, the radar operator's flight position is clearly visible. You can imagine how small the work space would have been with the canopy closed.

Inside the Arrow mock-up, looking aft, the photographer's position is right in the duct bay, just behind the centre section. Amazing details of the "Arrow guts," all made of wood, are visible. Note how packed the area between the engines was.

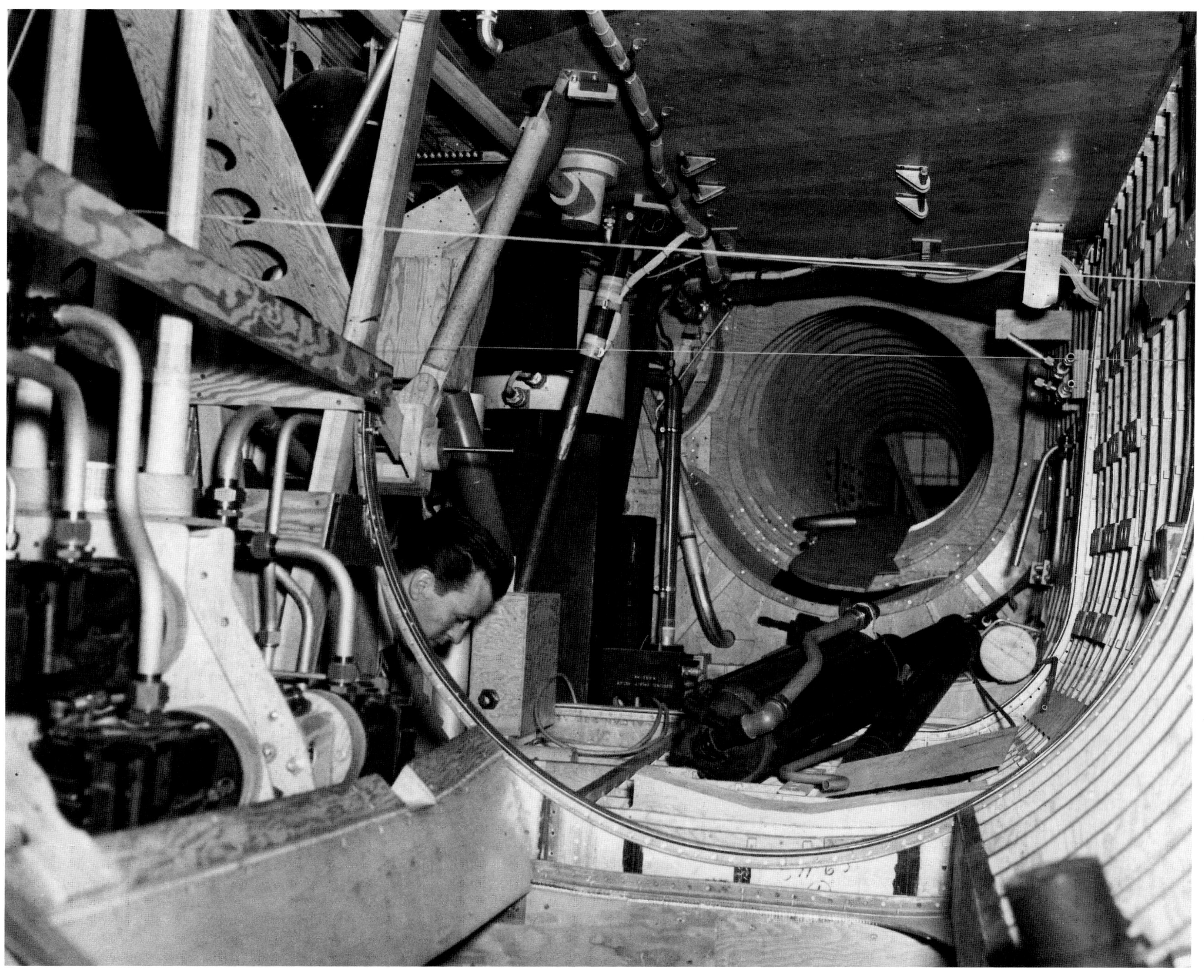

The photographer's position is now looking forward from the engine bay, right through the duct bay and centre section to the air intakes. Size is put into perspective with one of Avro's highly skilled carpenter's head popping up through the Hydraulic Access Panel.

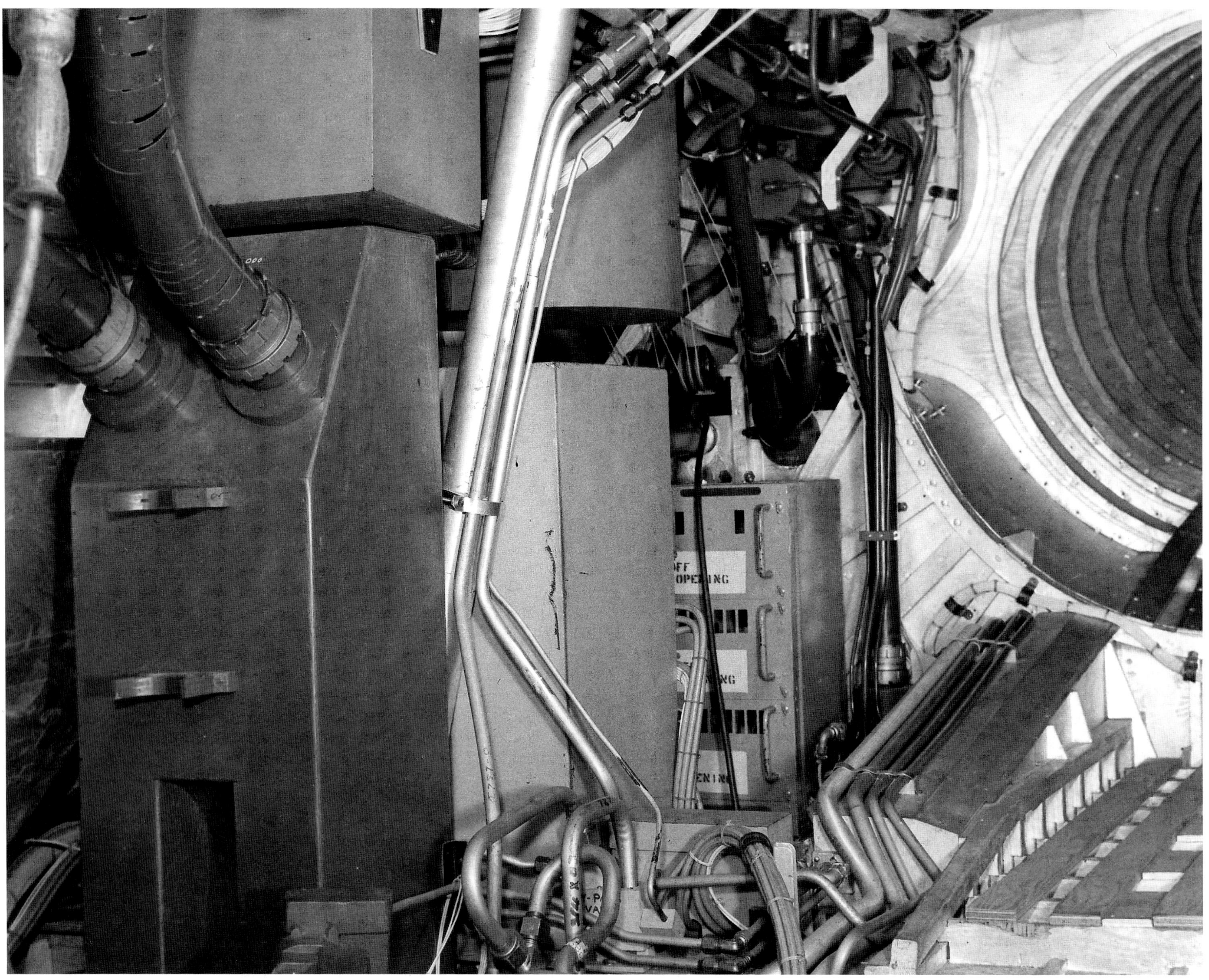

A closer look inside the Arrow wooden mock-up duct bay centre. Fuel to hydraulic fluid heat exchangers are visible. The upward sloping panel with pipes running up is the speed brake hydraulic jack housing.

Look at the detail and skill of the workmanship...this is all in wood! The whole main landing gear and stowage compartment have been assembled to scale.

Pilot visibility was of such concern that a modified truck and cockpit model was built to evaluate the envelope. Note the pipe adjusting positions to simulate various attitudes.

At high angles of attack forward visibility dropped off sharply. The aerodynamically required sharp front screen created distracting cross reflections. The USAF F102 and F106 suffered from the same defect. Their solution, a thin black central divider, solved the problem for them and us.

A great, "look down," view of the master models. Because the shape of the Arrow's skin was key to its performance, great care was given to making accurate models of any section that had any contact with air. Splashes could be taken from any area, tools created, parts made and verified, right back to these original models.

In Avro's bay #1 the Arrow metal mock-up takes shape. Since the Arrow was going to be built on production tooling from the start, the metal mock-up was required to make sure all parts came together within tolerance.

Anyone who has had the opportunity to stand, looking back, in the cockpit area of the mock-up, or for that matter the Arrow itself, has said, "One of the great Arrow views was the expanse of wing and its beauty that spread from front to rear, all 1,200 sq. ft. of it!"

Arrow WWW 000, the designation for the metal mock-up, was nearly a complete MK I aircraft. A detailed Pratt & Whitney J-75 mock-up is in the foreground, ready to be test fitted into the test airframe.

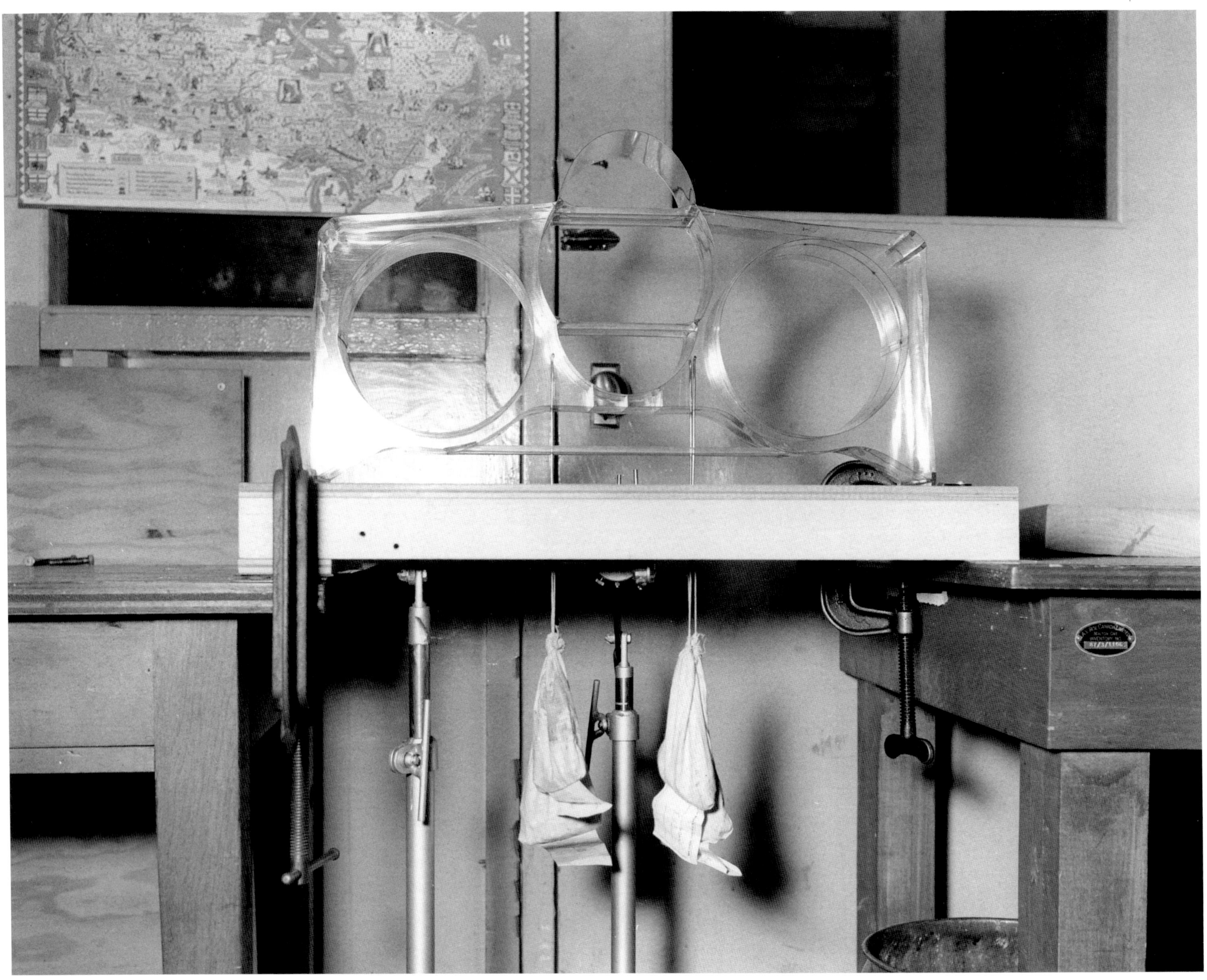

The whole Arrow program was interlaced with testing of all sorts. This particular photo shows a clear plastic model of a cross-section of the centre fuselage. Weights are applied at various key points and the whole piece is viewed through polarized light. Stress anomalies show up as distorted rainbow like patterns.

That production tooling referred to earlier is now taking shape. Rigid tubular frames supported jigs, clamps and guides. Theodolite measurements ensured accuracy and repeatability of a few thousands of an inch. Main reference points were the station numbers, in inches, beginning at the front of the airplane. For example the marry-up point of the front fuselage with the centre section was station number 255, or 255 inches from the zero point, near the front of the radome.

This sturdy looking jig was used to build the centre section bulk heads. This particular piece is from the left side looking forward. The various holes and clamps could accommodate all bulk heads both left and right.

A great view of the centre section from the front. The space between the two air tunnels housed the air conditioning equipment to keep the pilot, for the most part, cool. A water boiler, containing 200 lbs., was included to ensure cooling was still available at the extreme operating end of the flight envelope.

The aft bulkhead of the centre section, station number 485, was known as grand central. Many electrical, hydraulic, pneumatic and control items came together here. It joined the front of the aircraft to the back.

The weapons bay view of the same bulkhead. One of the key electrical junctions is mounted.

Fuel tanks 1 & 2 were placed between the two engine air intake tunnels and above the weapons bay. The top section of those tanks is being finished. The sloping front part supported the air conditioning cooling air duct. (That notch in the spine just behind the observer's position.)

This floating flexible duct connected the rigid centre section air tunnels to the suspended jet engines in the rear of the Arrow. They had blow out doors in the larger collar that can be seen near the bottom of the pipe. This was all part of the laminar flow control devices that brought as little disturbed air to the engines as possible.

John Wilson of sub-assembly is seen fabricating the stainless steel air conditioning duct that expelled used air, behind the observer's position, through the spine.

Engine nacelles are being assembled. The use of titanium in high temperature applications was pioneered by Avro and Orenda. The metal weighed half as much as steel and was just as strong. Because it could burn like magnesium when overheated, fabricators had to pay particular attention.

The Arrow nose section takes shape. Small assembly jigs progressed parts to larger and larger marry-up fixtures until a whole section was completed. The Arrow body was broken down into nose, centre, duct, and engine sections longitudinally.

The completed nose section of RL201 comes out of its jig. Note the two air brakes sitting on work-horses in the forefront of the photo.

Racks and racks of Arrow master pieces to be used as a reference in approving parts for movement on to the next production level. There were 38,000 parts in the Arrow. The administrative aspect of aircraft manufacturing can be appreciated in these photos.

Before the days of computers, record systems were bulky and required many people to maintain them. Of interest in this photo is the bin labeled nose section and the orderly method of keeping track of all the pieces, parts in progress, you name it! A complete paper trail and control system. You can see why 14,000 people were involved in building the Arrow.

Left and right inner wing completion jigs were situated at the north end of Avro's manufacturing Bay #1. The torsion box structure could be assembled and accessed through several stories as shown by the height of the fixtures in this photo.

RL201's completed, left side, inner wing comes out of the jig. Most of the enclosed volume was used as fuel tanks while a smaller portion housed the main landing gear.

The structural beam box shown was sandwiched between the two inner wings. The split fingers sticking up supported the Arrow's fin. Side lugs anchored the 4000 psi hydraulic system elevator jacks.

As the two wings come together in the inner wing marry-up jig, the fin beam box can be seen mounted in place. Note the centre section attachment bolts sticking out of the rear corners of the central forward space of the inner wings.

RL201's fin, with rudder control box in place, is fixed in its attachment jig. All internal wiring, cabling, hydraulic lines etc. are in place. The ends of the lines are hanging out of the bottom of the fin. The fin was lowered onto the vertical fingers and attached, in situ, by cross drilling the bolt holes.

The elevator takes shape after coming out of its assembly jig. The long piano hinge still needs to be attached, although the pivot point machinings are installed. Colecos everywhere!

There were more than 300 integrally machined parts in the Arrow. The elevator piano hinge was one of those and is shown being completed in this pantograph milling machine.

Duke Riggs, Avro's Vice President of Manufacturing, shows Orenda executives the complexity of some of the integrally machined parts of the Arrow. They see one of the Arrow's engine bay formers being machined out of one billet of aluminum...often more than 90% of the material was removed, to make the now lightweight part, and sold as scrap. Sam Lax had that contract too!

That same engine bay former just referred to, can now be seen as part of the finished engine bay which is being manipulated onto an inspection stand. Note all the access panel holes in this structure.

The Arrow's final marry-up jig in all its glory! Some posts contained a hydraulic cylinder which could be raised and lowered by the control box off to the far side. This way parts could be mated very gingerly. The wheeled frame in front, on the centre line track, brought the centre section in to the jig after the inner wing was positioned.

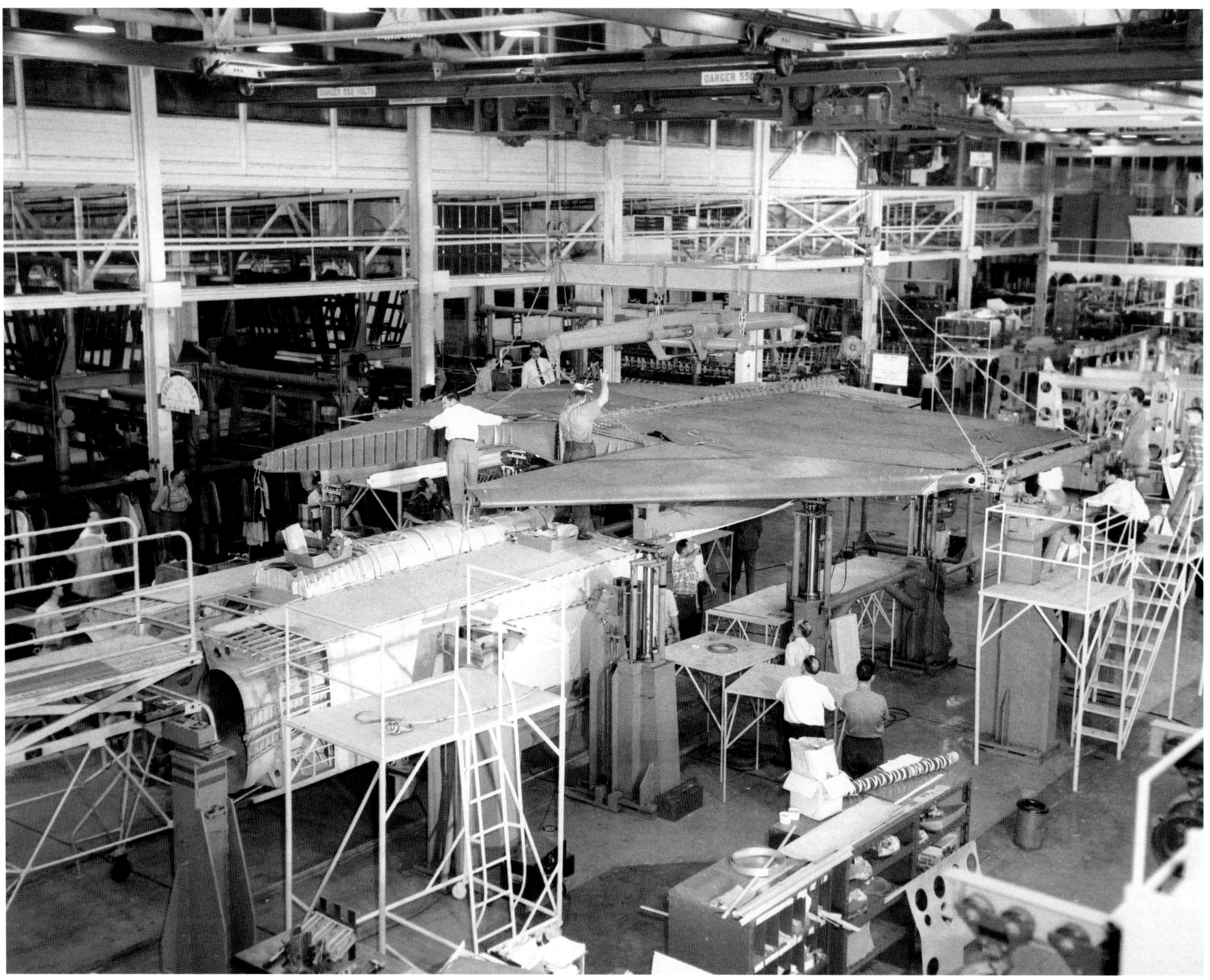

The inner wing of RL201 is being lowered onto the support points in the final marry-up jig. The centre section is available to be raised into place. Lots of white shirted management types are hovering around the workers as this first piece gets the treatment.

This vertical gantry carefully lowers the completed fin onto the back of the main wing structure. The attachment method is clearly seen at the junction. The anchoring bolts on the gantry can be adjusted so that the fin lowers and touches its matings point uniformly along its length.

The Arrow takes on its recognizable shape as the engine bay is pushed into place with the centrally aligned track and cart. A piano hinge connects the top end of the side walls to the bottom of the inner wing structure. The engines are suspended from the wing as well. The whole engine bay skin formed a forgiving flexible surface to absorb the buffeting and flexing of high speed flight, let alone the up and down pressures inside the engine compartments.

The rear fuselage engine and rudder faring uses the same track to align it with the engine bay before it too is attached.

Looking more and more like an Arrow, RL201 is pulled out of the final marry-up jig, ready for finishing.

A rear view of the Arrow, now able to stand on its own two feet. It just clears the works ceiling. Jan Zurakowski, the test pilot, fated to fly it within a year, walks briskly away.

Now final assembly can proceed in earnest. Crews wheel over the Dowty main gear and are getting ready to insert the forward pivot into its mating part just behind the eventual wing notch.

The outer wing assembly jigs look as big and imposing as the inner wing ones. Again, left and right wings are worked on simultaneously, side by side.

A close up of the inner wing assembly. The dropped leading edge is still open for inspection. The aileron hydraulic jack stowage compartment can just be made out in the bottom of the picture.

The finished inner wing is mounted on a special adjustable dolly. The outer wing is positioned and bolted by a but and lap joint covered with an aerodynamic faring.

Quality Control inspectors OK each step of the complex Arrow assembly. Here final adjustments are made to the right wing tip by Wally Grandey, left, and Bill Osborne of assembly.

Looking toward the rear of the Arrow, cockpit assembly under the guidance of Wilf Farrance takes shape. Again, because it is the first Arrow, many management types are hovering over the work.

The same view, but now looking south towards the Arrow's nose. The man in the foreground is standing in the yet to be equipped air conditioning bay. The shelf that will support the pilot's and observer's oxygen system is just in front of his waist.

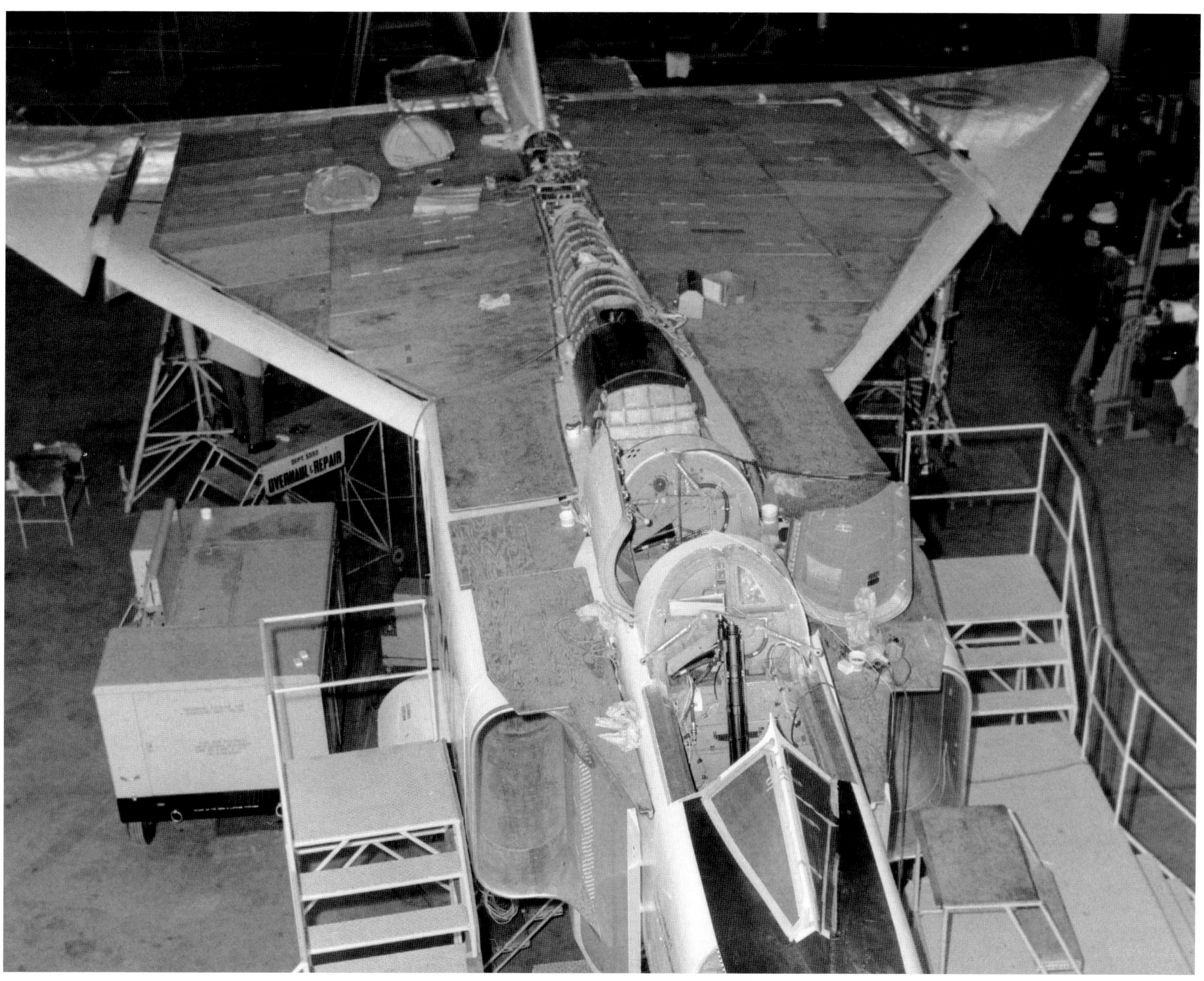

One of the finest views, in my opinion, of the Arrow in its last stages of final assembly. The delta wing dominates the image and lends weight to the pleasure of seeing it all behind you as you slowly turn to the rear while standing in the cockpit.

All of Avro's publications show attention to detail and good graphic design. This sample of the Rollout Ceremony agenda is no exception.

All VIPs were handed a full legal size folder containing copies of all VIP's names, titles etc.; copies of the speeches to be presented, an official agenda, a brochure detailing supersonic flight definitions; photos of the Arrow and its manufacture; and precis of the Arrow's development and research highlights.

The cover of the supersonic definition brochure...consistent design throughout!

Cover of the special commemorative Arrow Rollout publication. It detailed the manufacture and mission of the plane in great detail accompanied with many of the same photographs you see before you now!

Rollout dignitaries start to arrive. From left to right, Air Vice Marshall C.R. Dunlop, CBE, Bsc, Vice Chief of the Air Staff; J.A.D. McCurdy; Major General K. Berquist, Assistant Deputy Chief of Staff-Operations, USAF; A V/M L.E. Wray, Air Defence Command, RCAF; and General Leon Johnston, USAF, U.S. Representative, Nato Standing Committee. Is John McCurdy telling a fishing story?

Crawford Gordon gets into the fray!

Second from the left, W.R McLachlan, Executive Vice President A.V. Roe Canada Ltd.; Crawford Gordon, President and General Manager, A.V. Roe Canada Ltd.; and Sir Roy Dobson, Chairman of the Board, A.V. Roe Canada Ltd. and guests seem hyped up for the day's event.

The centre three figures from left to right are, A.V.M. Max M. Hendrick, Air Member for Technical Services, RCAF; Major General K. Berquist, USAF; J.S.D. Tory, Director, A.V. Roe Canada Ltd. The usual pre-show jokes and jitters. On the far left, A.V.M. J.G. Bryans, Air Officer Training Command

Harvey Smith, Vice President Manufacturing, Avro Aircraft Ltd.; A.V.M. C.R. Dunlap; and John McCurdy, the first man to fly a powered airplane in Canada, review the program handed out to invited guests.

A.V.M. L.E. Wray, AOC, Air Defence Command, RCAF and Jim Floyd are not discussing home cooked meals...I'll give you one guess!

VIP guests and A.V. Roe Canada Ltd. executives arrive to take their places on the podium. A hostess hands George Pearkes, Minister of National Defence, his official program.

The Arrow's main supporters and eventual dejectors come together on the platform to officiate the day's events. From left to right, General C. Foulkes, CB, CBE, DSO, MC, Croix de Guerre, Chief of Staff, Department of National Defence; Sir Roy Dobson, George Pearkes, Crawford Gordon and Fred Smye. You will note that I won't repeat all the personal titles and qualifications...just the first time.

Fred Smye gives the opening remarks and addresses thousands! He introduces Air Marshall Hugh Campbell, CBE, CD, US Legion of Merit, Degree of Commander, BSc., LLD, and Chief of the Air Staff.

SPEECH BY FRED T. SMYE

Remarks by Fred T. Smye, President and General Manager Avro Aircraft Limited, on the occasion of the unveiling of the Avro Arrow, October 4, 1957.

Mr. Minister, Honored Guests, Ladies and Gentlemen:

It is a great privilege to welcome you here this afternoon, on the occasion of moving the first Avro Arrow from the production line to the Flight Test hangar, and to its first public viewing. We are very grateful to think that you have taken the time to be with us to celebrate this event.

We feel particularly honored to have with us today the Minister of National Defence, and many other distinguished guests, some of whom are seated on the platform, and whom I would like to introduce to you.

A few words about the aircraft which you are about to see:

The Avro Arrow is a twin engine, long range, day and night supersonic interceptor. It has a crew of two. It is a big, versatile aircraft. The loaded weight of the Arrow is of the order of 30 tons.

The primary armament of the aircraft is to be air-to-air guided missiles, installed in a detachable armament bay in the fuselage. The versatility provided by this armament bay will enable the aircraft to perform other roles.

The aircraft will be equipped with one of the most advanced integrated electronics systems, which will combine the navigation and operation of the aircraft with its fire control system.

The Arrow is designed to operate from existing runways.

I believe it can be said that the Arrow is one of the most advanced combat aircraft in the world. It has been designed to meet the particular requirements of the Royal Canadian Air Force for the defence of Canada.

I wish to emphasize that this aircraft is by no means a handmade prototype, but that on the contrary it has been produced from very complete production tooling. This policy has been followed so that when the aircraft development has been completed, we will be able to move into the production phase without undue delay. Furthermore, an aircraft of the complexity and preciseness of the Arrow requires extensive tooling to ensure the accuracy of its manufacture.

This ceremony today is one of great significance to all of us at Avro, and we would like to think to the Canadian aviation industry. The Arrow, as you will shortly be seeing it, represents years of extremely hard work by our engineers, technicians, and craftsmen.

It is the result of constant probing into new and unknown technical areas to meet the ever-advancing requirements.

We feel that this aeroplane represents a substantial technical achievement, that it demonstrates the capability of Canadian technology, and represents a substantial Canadian contribution to the western world.

I cannot help but say how proud I am of the employees of Avro who have created what I think will become known, as a great aeroplane.

In this connection I would like to pay tribute to my colleagues, Mr. J.C. Floyd, Vice President of Engineering, and Mr. H. R. Smith, Vice President of Manufacturing, who have headed up their teams so admirably.

I would also like to pay tribute to the Canadian Government Agencies with whom we have worked so closely, and who have made such great contributions to this project. In particular, of course, I refer to the Royal Canadian Air Force, and to its staff of able technicians and engineers.

I also would like to make mention of the National Research Council, who have assisted in many technical areas, and particularly in the use of their wind tunnel and other test facilities.

The Department of Defence Production has also been a most helpful partner in this undertaking and is ever ready to assist us with our problems which arise in the sphere of their responsibility.

The Defence Research Board has likewise contributed its assistance in advice on technical

AVRO AIRCRAFT LIMITED

BOX 4004 TERMINAL 'A' TORONTO ONTARIO

Remarks by Fred T. Smye, President and General Manager
Avro Aircraft Limited,
on the occasion of the unveiling of the Avro Arrow,
October 4, 1957

Mr. Minister, Honored Guests, Ladies and Gentlemen:

It is a great privilege to welcome you here this afternoon, on the occasion of moving the first Avro Arrow from the production line to the Flight Test hangar, and to its first public viewing. We are very grateful to think that you have taken the time to be with us to celebrate this event.

We feel particularly honored to have with us today the Minister of National Defence, and many other distinguished guests, some of whom are seated on the platform, and whom I would like to introduce to you.

(Introduces guests.)

A few words about the aircraft which you are about to see:

The Avro Arrow is a twin engine, long range, day and night supersonic interceptor. It has a crew of two. It is a big, versatile aircraft. The loaded weight of the Arrow is of the order of 30 tons.

The primary armament of the aircraft is to be air-to-air guided missiles, installed in a detachable armament bay in the fuselage. The versatility provided by this armament bay will enable the aircraft to perform other roles.

The aircraft will be equipped with one of the most advanced integrated electronics systems, which will combine the navigation and operation of the aircraft with its fire control system.

The Arrow is designed to operate from existing runways.

problems, and greatly assisted the very important free flight model test program which was carried out at one of their facilities.

We also wish to say "thank you" to the United States Air Force and to the National Advisory Committee on Aeronautics for the co-operation and assistance which they have always been so free in offering.

Whereas the Arrow is an Avro product, and whereas we are responsible for the overall design and manufacture of the aircraft, we could be considered, let us say, as the captain of a team of hundreds of suppliers and sub-contractors who, together with us, did this job.

There are many companies who have made outstanding technical contributions in the design, development and manufacture of all types of equipment and material for the aircraft. To them I wish to express our deep appreciation and gratitude.

The first aeroplane which you will see today, and the next few development aircraft, will be powered with the Pratt & Whitney J75 engine. However, the ultimate engine to power the balance of the development aircraft, and all the production aircraft, is the recently unveiled Iroquois, designed by our associate company, Orenda Engines Limited.

As we have been creating the Arrow, they have been creating the Iroquois. This engine too represents a milestone in Canadian industrial accomplishment, and it is the thrust of this engine on which the very advanced performance of the Arrow will. depend.

At the close of this ceremony, the aircraft will be taken to the Flight Test hangar for flight preparation, which will involve exhaustive testing, and the installation of extensive, specialized instrumentation. The flight date of the aircraft will depend on the problems which will have to be dealt with during this phase of the program and, consequently, it is difficult to foretell. We are hopeful, however, that the aircraft will make its first flight before the end of the year.

Behind this first aircraft there are other, development aircraft in various stages of completion, and all of which will be subjected to an extensive and time-consuming flight test and development program. We know that, like all other aircraft of this type, where one is constantly probing the unknown, we will encounter many problems and setbacks and it will not be until this exhaustive testing is successfully concluded, and until the development phase of the program has been accomplished, that it will be able to see service in the squadrons of the Royal Canadian Air Force.

The CF100, which is currently in production for the Royal Canadian Air Force and the Belgian Air Force, was created, designed, developed and produced here at Malton. We like to feel that that aircraft has played an important role in the defence of our country, and has contributed to NATO. It is our fervent hope that, in due course, the Arrow will make the same contribution in the supersonic era in service with the Royal Canadian Air Force, and with the air forces of other, allied countries.

In closing, I would like to again thank the Royal Canadian Air Force and the Government of Canada for affording us the opportunity of designing both of these aircraft, and for entrusting to us this responsibility, of which we are so deeply conscious.

It is now my pleasure to introduce to you the newly-appointed Chief of the Air Staff, Air Marshal Hugh L. Campbell.

Air Marshal Campbell joined the Royal Canadian Air Force in 1931. Eleven years later, during World War II, he was posted overseas to the Royal Canadian Air Force Headquarters in England, as Director of Air Staff. In 1944 Air Marshal Campbell returned to Canada as Assistant Chief of the Air Staff.

In 1949 he was appointed Chairman of the Canadian Joint Staff, in Washington and, in that capacity, participated in the original work of the military committees of NATO. In 1952 Air Marshal Campbell was appointed Air Officer Commanding the Royal Canadian Air Force Air Division in Europe. He was the Commanding Officer during the building up of the Air Division in Europe# and earned international respect and admiration for himself and the Air Division in the carrying out of this important duty.

In August, 1955, he was appointed to the post of Deputy Chief of Staff Operations, at Supreme Headquarters Allied Powers Europe, more familiarly known as SHAPE. He filled this post with distinction and great credit to Canada until his appointment as Chief of the Air Staff on September 1st last.

Facing Page:
Some of the thousands that attended the rollout ceremony. In the original photo each face can be made out. Incredible photography!

Hugh Campbell gives his remarks to the multitude.

SPEECH BY AIR MARSHAL H. L. CAMPBELL

Address by
Air Marshal Hugh L. Campbell
Chief of the Air Staff
Avro Arrow roll-out ceremony,
Avro Aircraft Limited
Malton, Ontario - October 4, 1957.

Thank you Mr. Smye.

I am very grateful for this opportunity to participate in today's ceremony. It marks significant progress in the field of aviation. In particular the Arrow development is a forward step in the field of Canadian military aviation.

Suffice to say the planned performance of this aircraft is such that it can effectively meet and deal with any likely bomber threat to this continent over the next decade.

We in the Air Force look upon this aircraft as one component of a complex and elaborate air defence system covering in the first instance the whole of the North American continent, extending from Labrador to Hudson Bay to the Queen Charlotte Islands.

It is broader and wider than this continent. We are a member of a NATO alliance which comprises 15 nations. These nations, including Canada, have joined together in common defence and for the mutual protection of one another.

Its basic aim is to provide security for all its members. All have a common concept for defence.

It is Canada's belief that not only do we now have a greater collective strength for defence, but more important still, we are in a better position to deter aggression, that is a better position to convince a would be aggressor that war does not pay.

The air defence frontiers of this alliance extend from Alaska to Norway, to Germany, to Greece and Turkey, a perimeter distance of some 7,800 miles. The North American air defence system is a part of this overall air defence system of the NATO member.

An air defence system comprises aircraft and missiles, the ground environment of radar, whose mission it is to detect the enemy and to guide the path of our interceptors - - it comprises the communication links which tie together the radar sites, the command posts, the airfields and the missiles bases; it also includes the command structure which controls and exercises "the judgment" to fight the battle. All these many components, human, machine, organizational and technical are a part of and play an important role within any system.

Allied Command Europe now have and are in the process of building and expanding to a new and more powerful air defence system in their territory, extending from Norway to Turkey. We, as you are now aware, have an air defence system in North America. When they are all finished and linked together as one, covering the perimeter that I mentioned - - from Alaska to Turkey - - I think you will agree with me that it will make a great contribution to our deterrent to aggression.

This is the aim and objective of the military forces of NATO members. It is the aim and objective of the Royal Canadian Air Force that is, to deter aggression and prevent war.

The Arrow - including its missiles, flight trial and fire control systems - - we believe will become a very important component of this complex system. It has been designed to make a real contribution to the overall defence of North America.

Because this aircraft - - the Avro Arrow is a twin-engine, two-place machine - - and because it will embody what will be the most modern equipment in the airborne interception and fire control fields, it should have an inherent flexibility in operations and promising future development potential. For these reasons we look to it to fill a great need in the air defence system in the years to come.

I would like to pass on the thanks of the Royal Canadian Air Force to those who have contributed to the development of the Arrow, to those who have worked so hard to see it take shape.

To you Mr. Smye, the executive, and all the employees of Avro, you have our sincere appreciation. I would also like to endorse your remarks and pay tribute to the vast number of Canadians everywhere throughout the industrial complex of this nation who have contributed, and will continue to contribute towards this project.

AVRO AIRCRAFT LIMITED
BOX 4004, TERMINAL 'A', TORONTO, ONTARIO

Address by Air Marshal Hugh L. Campbell
Chief of the Air Staff
Avro Arrow roll-out ceremony, Avro Aircraft Limited
Malton, Ontario - October 4, 1957

Thank you Mr.Smye. I am very grateful for this opportunity to participate in today's ceremony. It marks significant progress in the field of aviation. In particular the Arrow development is a forward step in the field of Canadian military aviation.

Suffice to say the planned performance of this aircraft is such that it can effectively meet and deal with any likely bomber threat to this continent over the next decade.

We in the Air Force look upon this aircraft as one component of a complex and elaborate air defence system covering in the first instance the whole of the North American continent, extending from Labrador to Hudson Bay to the Queen Charlotte Islands.

It is broader and wider than this continent. We are a member of a NATO alliance which comprises 15 nations. These nations, including Canada, have joined together in common defence and for the mutual protection of one another.

Its basic aim is to provide security for all its members. All ~~for~~ have a common concept for defence.

It is Canada's belief that not only do we now have a greater collective strength for defence, but more important still, we are in a better position to deter aggression, that is a better position to convince a would be aggressor that war does not pay.

The air defence frontiers of this alliance extend from Alaska to Norway, to Germany, to Greece and Turkey, a perimeter distance of some 7,800 miles. The North American air defence system is a part of this

There are some 38,000 parts in this aircraft and over 650 companies in Canada have been engaged in their manufacture. In support also of this very considerable industrial complex has been the government organizations - - the Department of Defence Production, the Defence Research Board, the National Research Council, the National Aeronautical Establishment, and others.

I should also like to mention, as Mr. Smye has done, that a significant factor in this development has been the material interest and help received from the United States Air Force and the United States Navy, and from various American aeronautical research facilities. Special wind tunnels at Cornell University and at the NACA establishments in Langley Field and Cleveland have been made available to this Canadian project.

The development of the Arrow has been an outstanding piece of co-operation between service and industrial agencies on an international level. In acknowledging the assistance given by American agencies, I can but express the hope that the ultimate development of the Arrow will be the success that we expect it to be and that it will be accepted by them as a significant contribution to the defence of North America.

Today, we pass from one major phase to another in the growth of the Arrow. There are many difficult problems ahead -some can be foreseen, but some are hidden by the veil covering the unknown areas of aerodynamic science which has still to be explored. The phase that has been completed is an achievement in itself — but there is still a great deal — to be done before the aircraft we are to see today becomes the fighting machine which the Air Force requires for the air defence of Canada. The fact that so many previously unsolved technical problems have been overcome is assurance in itself that the problems of the future will be successfully surmounted.

To all of you who are engaged in the continuing task of this program we wish you God Speed - we shall follow your progress closely.

Hugh Campbell closes his remarks in a strange and most detached way.

Harry Graham, President of lodge 717 of the International Association of Machinists, was on the platform during rollout. It was he that got the greatest cheer from the crowd because just hours before the ceremony a new work contract had been reached with Avro Aircraft.

"It is a distinct honor, and a great pleasure, for me to now introduce the Minister of National Defence, the Honorable George R. Pearkes, V.C."

"We deeply appreciate the fact that he has generously consented to officiate at this ceremony today. His outstanding record of service and devotion to his country is well known to all of you. Therefore, without further delay, I wish to call upon the Honorable George R. Pearkes, V.C. the Minister of National Defence."

SPEECH BY HON. GEORGE R. PEARKES, V. C.

Address by the Honorable George R. Pearkes, VC.,
Minister of National Defence
Avro Arrow roll-out ceremony, Avro Aircraft Limited,
Malton, Ontario - October 4, 1957.

Fifty years ago a great Canadian pioneer, John McCurdy, flew the Silver Dart, the first aircraft in Canada, in fact it was the first heavier-than-air plane to fly in the British Commonwealth. History recognizes that event as the beginning of Canada's air age. This event today marks another milestone — the production of the first Canadian supersonic aeroplane. I am sure that the historian of tomorrow will regard this event as being equally as significant in the annals of Canadian aviation.

The supersonic era of flight is just beginning. Many of today's aircraft are regularly breaking the sound barrier, but this is done at the extreme peak of their performance. Supersonic flight is still not a routine matter. Present aircraft travel at these exceptionally fast speeds for a relatively short period of time. The Avro Arrow, however, has been designed from the outset to operate supersonically throughout as much of its mission as is deemed necessary. It will be equally at home at one side of the sound barrier as on the other. It will be a truly supersonic aircraft.

It is difficult for the layman to appreciate the magnitude and complexities of the problems of the last four years culminating in this first phase of the Arrow project. Four years ago the Air Force and the industry set out together on a voyage into the unknown. All the technical difficulties which have been solved thus far have represented pioneering work in aerodynamics, metallurgy, mechanics and electronics and in all the related arts and sciences which form part of our aeronautical industry. Thus far progress has been commendably rapid. We are, of course, only part way along the road and no-one would be so foolish as to suggest that the job is complete by any means.

Four years of design, testing, tooling and production problems lie behind. Many months of further tests, trials, complex development and modification lie ahead before this aircraft can be considered operationally acceptable. I understand it will be some years yet before this supersonic aircraft with its missile and guidance systems will be available for operational use. We are looking forward to this time.

It is important to appreciate the significance of proper timing in the introduction of weapons under today's conditions. Our weapons must not only be designed to be better than those of unfriendly nations, they must be ready in time to counteract those weapons should the need arise. If either the timing is wrong or the quality is wrong, we fail to maintain the proper balance of power in our goal towards presenting the most effective deterrent.

AVRO AIRCRAFT LIMITED
BOX 4004 TERMINAL 'A' TORONTO ONTARIO

Address by the Honorable George R. Pearkes, VC.,
Minister of National Defence
Avro Arrow roll-out ceremony, Avro Aircraft Limited,
Malton, Ontario - October 4, 1957

Fifty years ago a great Canadian pioneer, John McCurdy, flew the Silver Dart, the first aircraft in Canada, in fact it was the first heavier-than-air plane to fly in the British Commonwealth. History recognizes that event as the beginning of Canada's air age. This event today marks another milestone - - the production of the first Canadian supersonic aeroplane. I am sure that the historian of tomorrow will regard this event as being equally as significant in the annals of Canadian aviation.

The supersonic era of flight is just beginning. Many of today's aircraft are regularly breaking the sound barrier, but this is done at the extreme peak of their performance. Supersonic flight is still not a routine matter. Present aircraft travel at these exceptionally fast speeds for a relatively short period of time. The Avro Arrow, however, has been designed from the outset to operate supersonically throughout as much of its mission as is deemed necessary. It will be equally at home at one side of the sound barrier as on the other. It will be a truly supersonic aircraft.

It is difficult for the layman to appreciate the magnitude and complexities of the problems of the last four years culminating in this first phase of the Arrow project. Four years ago the Air Force and the industry set out together on a voyage into the unknown. All the technical difficulties which have been solved thus far have represented pioneering work in aerodynamics, metallurgy, mechanics and electronics and in all the related arts and sciences which form part of our aeronautical industry. Thus far progress has been commendably rapid. We are, of course, only

I would like to recognize the great number of Canadians in our industry who have contributed and will continue to contribute towards this project. I would also like to thank the personnel of those American agencies who have helped so materially in the aircraft's development. As the Chief of Staff has said, the development of the Arrow has been an outstanding piece of co-operation between the service and industrial agencies on an international level.

Much has been said of late about the coming missile age and there have been suggestions from well-intentioned people that the era of the manned aeroplane is over and that we should not be wasting our time and energy producing an aircraft of the performance, complexity and cost of the Avro Arrow. They suggest that we should put our faith in missiles and launch straight into the era of push-button war. I do not feel that missiles and manned aircraft have, as yet, reached the point where they should be considered as competitive. They will, in fact, become complementary. Each can do things which the other cannot do, and for some years to come both will be required in the inventory of any nation seeking to maintain an adequate "deterrent" to war. However, the aircraft has this one great advantage over the missile. It can bring the judgment of a man into the battle and closer to the target where human judgment, combined with the technology of the aircraft, will provide the most sophisticated and effective defence that human ingenuity can devise.

The aircraft now being produced in the various countries of our NATO alliance may or may not be the last of the manned interceptors. With the rapid strides being made in the fields of science and engineering, it would be unwise to attempt to forecast the future in this respect. However, I feel sure that if these aircraft continue their development with the same promise as they have in the past, there is no doubt in my mind that they will be a necessary requirement to the arsenal of the West for many years to come.

In closing, I would like once again to commend the efforts of those who have contributed thus far to the development and production of this airplane. Through your efforts you are making a direct contribution to the defence of the free nations of the world and so to the well-being of us all.

I now have pleasure in unveiling the Avro Arrow as Canada's first supersonic aircraft - a symbol of a new era for Canada in the air.

George Pearkes concludes his remarks in an up-beat way by complimenting all who have contributed to the program and to the defence of the free nations of the world.

George Pearkes pulls the cord that opens the hangar curtain... "I now have the pleasure in unveiling the Avro Arrow—as Canada's first supersonic aircraft—a symbol of a new era for Canada in the air." What a symbol the Arrow was, became, and could be again!

You can imagine the tension and pride that would be inside everyone there as the Arrow, in all its majesty, pokes its nose out of the hangar for the first time. Wow! What a shot.

The Air Force Band strikes up "March Past," the official anthem of the RCAF. CF-100s fly low over the crowd symbolizing a generational hand-over.

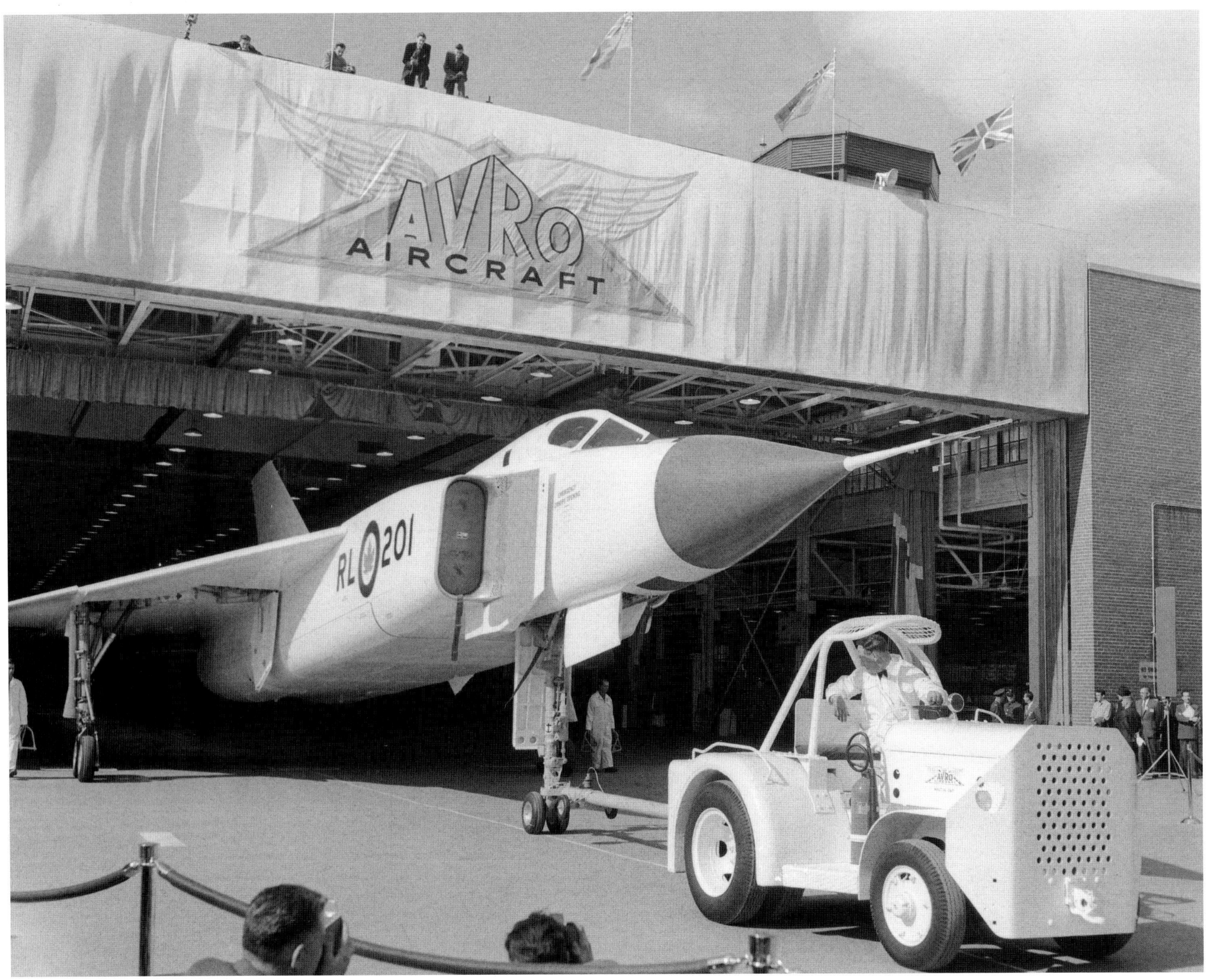

The first classic Arrow rollout photo. What framing and composition. The Arrow is as beautiful today as it was then.

Jim Floyd, just beaming as his baby sees the light of day!

Looking east, with the sun on our back, the Arrow's rollout is nearly complete. What would you give to go back in time and share the tremendous joy within all those present, that magic day, 45 years ago?

A bit more of a long view taken from the press bleachers by the parking lot fence.

The Arrow provided great photo opportunities from any angle.

It doesn't take long before dignitaries decide it's time to go. The limousines are waiting.

Again, from left to right, A.V.M., Max Hendrick; CAS, Hugh Campbell; John Tory; DND Chief of Staff, Charles Foulkes; Wilf A. Curtis, AM retired, Vice Chairman of the Board, A.V. Roe Canada Ltd. Probably there was a reception to go to at Briarcrest , the company retreat at Dixon and Islington.

This is the first picture that had a caution across it. "Do not print, as per the RCAF." Who was this couple, obviously VIP's, but who?

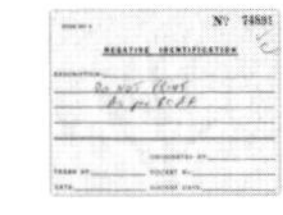

A mass scene, looking west, in which, if you look carefully, you can pick out most of the key players such as Jim Floyd, Fred Smye, George Pearkes, Hugh Campbell, John McCurdy, etc.

No introduction is needed to these executives. The young man on the right is Crawford Gordon's son Crawford. What an occasion and privilege to be there and have your dad running the place.

Lots of chit chat...after all this was an exciting moment.

The Arrow's main landing gear complexity and size is being studied and admired by enthusiastic on-lookers.

One of the key features of the Arrow's intakes was the 12 degree shock ramp ensured that slower than mach 1.0 air speed entered the throat of the engines. Boundary layers everywhere, were removed by suction and by-pass, for optimal efficiency.

There is mutual respect but Mr. X seems to be leading George Pearkes. Does anyone know who mr. X is? Some say , because of the vest that he must have been British.

The crowds are starting to thin out. The ceremony is starting to wind down. These roof shots really capture our imagination.

A small private plane flies over the crowd and takes some great pictures, like the one following. It's interesting that another small private plane, some 20 months later, would reveal to the world that the Arrow was to be no more and was being secretly destroyed.

This is a great view from a light aircraft that somehow managed to get over the Avro plant during the Rollout Ceremony. The Arrow's massive proportions are clearly visible as hundreds still mill about—admiring their accomplishment.

Another well framed shot from the roof. Note the bleacher for the official photographers and further back, on the taxi way, a USAF transport plane that brought their VIPs.

The official day is over and Harry Beffort, Production Shop Manager, is relieved as his smile to the camera shows. Note the clump of people near the port side main gear - can you make out Jan Zurakowski?

The crowd is now mostly gone. The hangar doors to Bay#1 are closing. It's time for official photographs at the west end of the taxi way. Once again the tow-motor is attached and white-suited escorts surround the Arrow as it moves west.

Photographers Beware! The Arrow starts its journey, first to the west for official photos and then off to the D2 hangar to be prepped for taxi and flight trials.

A visiting Soviet delegation member once remarked that it was impossible to have that many cars just for employees...it must have been staged to exaggerate the wealth of the average worker.

A USAF transport, near the horizon, waits for their delegation.

A real "Runway Model" poses for official photographs!

25201
RL 201

This is a great photo showing exactly how thin the wings really were. What a view and yes, all that gear could be stowed, amazing....

In my opinion, this is one of the most dramatic photos of the lot. Two RCAF pilots pay homage to their future which, for all they knew, included the Arrow. Dust clouds swirl in the background—portent of future woes! There's an air of mystery and hope. No wonder the RCAF said "Do not print as per the RCAF."

Just one more photo, film, or comment and then it's off to the D2 hangar to unfold a new phase of the Arrow story. The route: north on the west taxi-way curve around the east, north again past the experimental D1 hangar, turn around, back it up, and in she goes!

Backing the Arrow into the D2 Hangar was tricky business.

Watch those wing tips.

The day behind them, Crawford Gordon and Sir Roy Dobson have every reason to be jubilant... expecting good media coverage was natural...but it was not to be...!

The Bosses and Brass have left without a hassle...not so for the everyday bloke...traffic jams at the exit were common every day. What a collectors dream to have this many vintage cars at his disposal at one time....

Only small coverage on page 5 of the Globe & Mail gives credence and homage to the Rollout of the world's fastest jet fighter/interceptor. The launching of Sputnik overnight shadows the need for the Arrow and gets big headlines. Even though a large picture of the Arrow is on the front page it clearly portents events to come. Too bad!

WEEKLY

The Globe and Mail

Partly Cloudy; High 60

Detailed Weather Report on Page 2

...an Edition — TORONTO, SATURDAY, OCTOBER 5, 1957. — 10 Cents Per Copy—Carrier Delivery 40 Cents Weekly — 158 PAGES

RUSSIA LAUNCHES FIRST SATELLITE

Past Toronto Already, Expert Says

The world's first man-made satellite, fired into space yesterday by Russia, probably passed over Toronto last night in its 90-minute orbit, a scientist said.

Moscow Radio reported Russian physicists sent a 180-pound sphere spinning around earth, perhaps paving the way to in-

Paves Way To Planets,

...ersonic Interceptor — Canada's first faster-than-sound jet interceptor is ... from its Avro Aircraft Ltd. hangar at Malton for its first ... appearance. The Arrow, formerly the CF-105, can carry a hydrogen bomb or an arsenal of guided missi... mph. All-weather plane was seen by a num... aviation designers and engineers from all pa...

Expect RCAF To Get 39 of 1,500-MPH Jets For Missile Missions

Two advanced jetfighter aircraft which will probably be the nation's first line of defence for the next decade were unveiled yesterday at Avro Aircraft's Malton plant.

Practically all eyes at yesterday's impressive ceremony marking the unveiling of Avro's revolutionary CF-105 were rivetted to the unusual-looking, delta-wing superjet which is expected to fly around 1,500 mph while carrying either an atomic weapon or a deadly nest of air-to-air Sparrow missiles. The RCAF is reported ready to place about four years—announced its appearance by an ear-shattering sonic boom as it dipped low in salute to the aircraft which will doom it to obsolescence.

Mark VI Not Mentioned

Recently rumors were rife that the Canadian government was going to scrap the transonic Mark VI program to save almost $200,000,000 in defence costs, and gamble on the slower Mark V's until the supersonic CF-105's were proven and produced in quantity.

In unveiling the CF-105 yes-

Each can ... other can ... years to ... quired in ... nation se... adequate ...

Advan...

An airc... (which A... Arrow), s... had an ad... sile in th... judgment ... and close... human ju... the techn... will prov... cated and ... human in...

Air Ma... the RCAF ... staff, said ... would b... bomber t... that migh... decade.

Present... veiled ye... of overh... moving s... "March P...

TORONTO DAILY STAR: Saturday, Oct. 5, 1957 5

10,000 Marvel at CF-105, Almost Miss Mark VI at Malton

THE NEW 30-TON CANADIAN FIGHTER, CF-105 Avro Arrow, was unveiled at Malton by Hon. George Pearkes, minister ... "Mach two" speed, which means anything from 1,200 to 1,600 mph. depending on height and atmosphere. Avro's CF-105

THE GLOBE AND MAIL, SATURDAY, OCT. 5, 1957. 5

Supersonic Flights Routine to Arrow, Defense Head Says

The supersonic Arrow—sleek, fast and deadly—was unveiled yesterday at Malton. Canadian designed and built, it is one of the world's most advanced high altitude all-weather interceptors.

Defense Minister Pearkes, VC

Defense Minister Pearkes, VC, told 2,000 guests including many air attaches from Ottawa's diplomatic corps and aviation designers and engineers from all parts of the world:

"The supersonic era of flight is just beginning. Many of today's aircraft are regularly breaking the sound barrier, but this is at the extreme peak of their performance and supersonic flight is still not a routine matter.

"The Arrow, however, has been designed from the outset to operate supersonically throughout as much of its mission as is necessary. It will be equally at home on one side of the sound barrier as on the other. It will be a truly supersonic aircraft."

Several thousand Avro Aircraft Ltd. workers who have been working on the project in the past four years cheered as the 34-ton, 1,600 mph white plane rolled out of its closely guarded hanger.

This first model, built almost entirely of titanium and other specially blended metals to withstand tremendous friction, was minus its array of guided missiles which will give it the hitting power of a destroyer's broadside.

Air Marshal H. L. Campbell, Chief of the Air Staff, said:

"We look to the Arrow to fill a great need in the air defense system."

He said it will have a specific role when the North American and European air defense systems are linked.

Speaking of defense needs and advances, Pearkes stated:

"Much has been said about the coming missile age and there have been suggestions that the era of the manned airplane is over and we should not be wasting our time and energy producing an aircraft of the performance, complexity and cost of Arrow. They suggest we should put our faith in missiles and launch straight into the era of push-button war.

"I do not feel that missiles and manned aircraft have, as yet, reached the point where they should be considered as competitive. They will in fact become complementary. Each can do things which the other cannot do, and for some years to come both will be required on the inventory of any nation seeking to maintain an adequate deterrent to war."

Similarly, the Toronto Star pushes the Arrow story to page 5. We can imagine the disappointment of all Avroites and Orendaites as they receive their Saturday paper.